Some things just shouldn't.

Kate Barden

BookLeaf Publishing

Presentation by *BookLeaf Publishing*

Web: www.bookleafpub.com

E-mail: info@bookleafpub.com

ISBN: 978-93-95784-09-2

First edition 2022

DEDICATION

To Lil and Amelie, and Hope x

ACKNOWLEDGEMENT

... lovely family and courageous friends; your shit experiences are in here and I thank you for sharing them.

... endlessly patient love of my life, Steve; "til one of us dies" (and that'll be a shit thing); I thank you for everything, always.

PREFACE

Shit things happen. Sometimes we look back and realise that it was obvious that something shit was going to happen, and maybe we shouldn't have done what we did.... but sometimes something really bad happens that is out of our control, and it utterly and completely knocks us over. This book isn't some sort of spiritual guide, and it DEFINITELY ISN'T going to say 'things happen for a reason' (if anyone ever says that, walk away, quickly...they are bad people to have around). This is a collection of poems about some shit things, some of which happened to me and some which happened to my dear friends and family. It is my hope that one of them, or at least a line or a few words, will go a tiny way towards acknowledging your pain and saying, 'I hear you'.

My person

Life was mistakes
heartbreaks
full of fakes…

and then I met you
and in 6 months,
give or take
it's real; we're awake... and
I say yes.
You pass the test of my tribe,
accepted, voted in by a landslide.
I won't deny my pride, asked to be your bride
I make it official on the web, worldwide.
Spring and summer bring sunshine, swimming,
love and laughter.

But we weren't ready for the winter tide,
diagnosis caught us on a blindside
took our feet, left us stranded, drowning and
falling
with no warning…

so no snow white gown and no decorated aisle
just yet
instead it's green scrubs and a bleached corridor

you're dignified
allied, as this love of ours
fortifies
against nature's homicide
and for now that is enough
for today,
for one step at a time
until the stars realign
and I am yours and you are mine;
my person.

Incentives

Go and make something of yourself, they said,
finish school, get a job.
There's a good brain in that head.

Work hard, they said, you'll go far.
Start at the bottom
before you know it, you'll be in charge.

Show commitment, they said. Bit more time
you'll get noticed,
get promoted, boss will see you shine.

Start early, finish late, they said,
didn't harm us,
working til our fingers bled.

Drag yourself in, they said. You'll be fine.
You're not that sick.
You need the overtime.

Employee of the month; top member of the
crew,
they said, will get a bonus.
Who are you?

Venus

5

... suspended,
you wait, seemingly doing nothing
and without movement you attract all you need.
How wondrous you are,
a deep, killing machine;
once in, there's no escape,
tricked by the perfume,
lured by the prospect of warmth and
nourishment,
teetering on the edge
then falling into you
unable to escape
until drowned...
... and suspended,
you wait, seemingly doing nothing.
How dangerous you are, Venus.

Lessons

7

These are lessons, someone says.
Fuck you, I say,
shit happens
and it shouldn't.

What?

They tell me it's Tuesday.

It's Wednesday, mum,
we're going to the shop, remember?

You are still there.
I know you are.
In the glimmer of your eyes
in the tilt of your head
the young you shines.
We sing show tunes

the words, learnt 65 years ago,
come dancing easily from your lips
your red lipstick once so carefully applied
to a perfect cupids bow
now a redundant mystery object
held in the palm of your hand
and looked at in puzzlement
you wouldn't know what to do with it
in a million years.

Let me.
Do this.

What are you doing with your... what's it... mouth, silly girl?
Now, where's my hat... Sundays are church days.

It's Wednesday, mum,
we're going to the shop, remember?

You are still there.
I know you are.
With the soft touch of your hand
with the kind smile
the young you shines.
Your shoes don't match
and are on the wrong feet;
you don't notice,
at least you know roughly where they go
most of the time

Let me just...

Get off my whatcha call em, silly girl.
Where's my hat? Friday is fish for tea.

It's Wednesday, mum,
we're going to the shop, remember

You are still there.
 I know you are.
Your red beret sits atop you,
complete with unplanned jaunty angle
and you are efficient, 35, busy,
going to work, looking after us,
doing all the things mum does

without complaint, with love.
The young you shines.
In the kiss on my cheek
in the skippity skip down the path
la la la-ing songs from the shows

Quick, we'll miss the bus!
Saturday is for dancing!

It's Wednesd...
yes, mum, Saturday is for dancing.

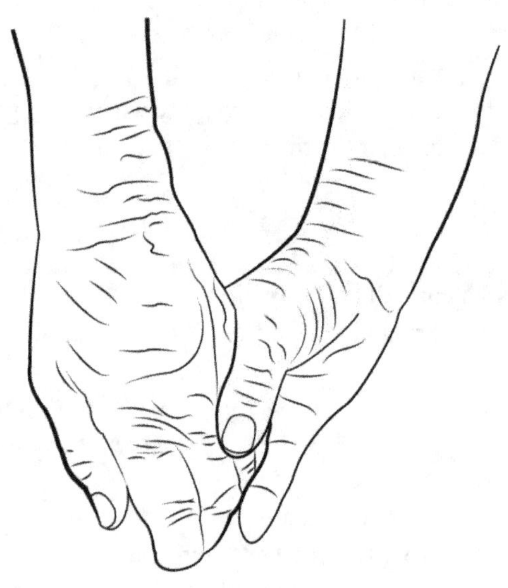

3am

At 3am my phone rings, vibrates next to my
head.
I'm in bed.
Instant dread....... breathe.
Who rings at 3am?
'The police are on their way.'
Knock knock knock
I don't have to stop all the clocks
3am stands still on its own
I stand still, alone.
The world has stopped....... breathe.
At 3am the world has stopped and I don't know
if it will ever start again and nor do I care
at 3am my heart is shattered into sharp
fragments
and cast around the world..... breathe.
 I am like the Snow Queen
as my once warm heart is frozen into icey
daggers.
My chest is full of icey daggers
at 3am.
Breathe..... breathe....
at 3am, words are delivered from the young
mouth of a young policeman, sitting on the edge
of my dark sofa in my dark lounge and

at 3am my dark lounge fills with words I can't
hear and
I am underwater and nothing makes sense and
there is no clear way up and out..... breathe.
3am is still, still, still and dark.
I collect clothes.... breathe.... car keys....
breathe.... dog barks....
breathe.... as my icy dagger heart tries to cut its
way out....
breathe.... be practical, people to tell.... and
breathe.... then go to her.
At 3am I held my breath.... and now
my heart is broken
and it will forever
be
3am.

Chrysalis

It didn't emerge, the butterfly
it didn't have chance to grow
it started life
contained and safe
as one they were yet to know.

Enclosed and warm, in darkness it lay
with love, inside its cocoon,
gently rocking
as whispered winds
murmured through the nurturing womb.

As loved as any that came before
in tranquil bliss held close,
the precious life
cared not for time, nor future
bringing joy and hope.

Perfect where it was, the pupa lay unseen
the uninterrupted,
peaceful, being
just as it should have been

and when the pain came searing down
and spread within and through,
there was no precious butterfly.
and we cried, because we knew

it couldn't emerge, the butterfly
it didn't have chance to grow
it started life
contained and safe
as one we were yet to know.

The Lonely

The sea is
my place, the space
where I can hide safe
body and face
          (cover cuts, release the harm, conceal
picked skin, scarred thigh, cut arm)
          (the years of doubt and forced calm
squashed inside)
          (only released with a slice from a knife)

no judgement under the sea
covered up, being real
the chance to feel
a different pain
to freeze my brain

it   frees   my   brain
(hard to explain)
(the shame, self-blame)
(the blood of doubt flows through my veins)
(thedeadheadthatfeelsnothingandtoomuchandnot
hingallatonce...because on top of every frantic
thing else I don't want to go today...)

but go I must, I know I must, go I must, I know I
must, go the pain's decreased
piece by fragile piece
through peaceful swimming, self belief's increased
and as the sea moulds to my body
my body unfolds
tingling   stinging   singing   bringing
all my senses back to it for moments of pure joy
saved by waves
from an early grave
this place, my safe brave space
where the constant routine
of the marine
heals the unseen
and is serene
it comes in and goes out comes in and goes out
reassuringly the same
day after day hypnotically
therapeutically the tranquility
of my place
brave space
   where I embrace, safe, body and face.

Broken wheel

It was dark and the wheel squeaked, turning
slowly.
It was all anyone would hear
if they'd been near
but the street was empty.
A cat jumped onto the wall above my head
a rat sniffed vegetable peelings and dog piss next
to the bin
and I lay on the ground
the tarmac cold
hard against my back
the clattering came from foxes
they thought
those tucked up in bed who knew not what was
happening...

His fist had come from nowhere, struck
me
to the pavement,
my bike to the wall
with such force
the wheel buckled
I snatched short gasps of air
as under his weight

I was repulsed by his hot breath
filthy with tobacco and beer.

My broken wheel squeaked...
He grunted, heaved, came and left, the sound of
his footsteps
followed by the sound of throaty wailing
bouncing from wall to wall and gate to gate
foxes they said...

This is the street where I live
where I walk or ride my bike every day
where I say good morning to neighbours
where I wave cheerfully.

Lying in the gutter
there were no stars to stare at,
no light, barely even a glow from the sallow
streetlight in the next alley,
the town clock struck
I couldn't count how many
and my broken wheel stopped spinning.

The bruises faded
I didn't ride my bike again
and I agreed that the foxes were becoming a
nuisance.

The push me pull you

Where does it go?
Where the fuck does it go?
Actually I know.
You let it go.
You pushed it so hard it had to go. It left.
It walked out. And came back a bit
and left again.
Too great, the pain.
Shattered, broken, tired,
couldn't get back up and couldn't fight anymore.
Be quiet! Hear me. Listen to me.
Too late; too much and too little at the same
time.
An enormous love lies lost,
a little left in the bottom of the glass,
smells the same as before and with rose tints
looks like it might revive and become the
full-bodied richness it was.
But then you push and pull and bend and stretch
and it can't survive that.
Not now.
After all this.

Things conspire

You stub your toe
you drop a glass
you trip in town
fall on your ass
you break a nail
you stand in shit
you trip in town
you look a tit
you lose your card
you miss your train
you trip in town
your ankles sprained.
you're late for work
you drop your keys
you trip in town
you graze your knees
you ladder your tights
you trip in town
you get a cold
your internet is down
your cat is dead
you trip in town
your partner leaves
you just stay down
cos getting up is just too much…

Alanis said these things are all ironic
and although that idea give her a hit,
some things in life conspire against you
and simply, are nothing else but
shit.

What's mine's my own safe place?

I say I am one thing
or another
English, female, white
a certain weight, a certain height
but these descriptions sometimes trap me,
make me distinct, just one divided, apart from
you.
Make what's mine my own
and not for sharing
individual,
has no bearing
on other people.
What's mine is my own
and I keep my own close
the fear of losing who I am and what I am and
where I am,
but the labels
come to haunt me
keep me separate
used to taunt me
by me, myself
the self, the only one and only
a sense of being
sense of being skinnier and boney

and flesh and blood thicker than water
a mum, a dad, a son, a daughter.
What's mines my own
my tribe, my prison
keeps me out
keeps me in
a fence around the pretty garden
look at my flowers... from a distance
I grew them and they're just for me
don't stop to look
or stop for love
it might not start
it might not fit
best not to risk it...
and so describe myself in 3 words
and shut the door
stay inside
and give the self
a sense of pride.

Lifted

We had three there yesterday.
Are you sure?
Three, and now there is one
and no record of them being sold.
Ripped off, conned
they saw us coming
and they took without paying,
no respect.
I blame the parents
blame rap music
blame the media
blame the police
blame society
blame the weather

and lying on his dirty blanket
eyes closed,
a drop of golden cider
decorated his stinking beard.

He took it

He took it from me
and I let him,
misguided, stupid, naïve.
The light
the soul
the spirit
I put the man first before love for myself
a false loyalty
lost in a notion of romance,
the stories told to me as a child
lost in a dream of love and
compromise.
He took it from me
and I let him,
opportunity, future dreams
swapped for a life lived in fear,
fear of hurting, fear of being hurt;
the bravery and courage which remains,
a shadow of the love
that he took from me
and I let him.

Rocked by the sea

We went around there, a few years ago,
around the rocks where nobody else existed
where we could take off our clothes and feel the
sun on our bodies.
I know the glorious warmth on my skin
dancing across my breasts
dancing across your chest, your tummy.
The cormorants stand guard, soldiers protecting
their castle;
a kayak glides by, slow, lazy strokes
slow, lazy gentle strokes, my hand on yours
blue skies, grey-green eyes.
Here I am now
at the point; the castle; the rocks; the sea;
and although you are not here,
I know the heat of the sun,
and I still feel it dance on my body.

Baggage

I'm not much good in company
I never come alone
I bring my baggage with me
and then I drag it home
my suitcase wheels behind me
hold-all that's not for outings
stuffed full of life's experiences
insecurities, self-doubtings
the handbag that I carry
bulging at the seams
is stuffed with the residue of trauma
of flashbacks and bad dreams
I cram things in my satchel
and wear it into town
it's slung over one shoulder
the contents weigh me down
I might swap it for my rucksack
filled with life's shit bric-a-brac
but this drags my shoulders downwards
and weighs heavy on my back
for posh events there's my valise
portmanteau for nice trips
zipped up tight, triggers contained within
my emotional bag of tricks

and if you see me with my purse,
you'll know right now that life's alright
the least intrusive of my bags
this one's nice and light.
It doesn't matter what the gathering,
my baggage comes along
love me and love my luggage
their weight has made me strong.

Bluebells

The bluebells are coming,
their beauty a portent for the whirling spinning
giddiness of grief
their nodding bells signaling the hole in the
season
opening up the ground and the sky
into which I fall.
The bluebells are coming and they catch me by
surprise,
it's only March.
They march, blue uniformed soldiers
into April and then
it's May and
they're still here
bending, bobbing, nodding, knowing.
They tease and taunt with their happy go lucky
'here I am popping up all over the place-ness',
tainting the joy of the sun
cleverly disguised as gloriousness
reflecting their blueness
onto the dry muddy path.
I can't stop the bluebells from coming.
I hate them for my powerlessness against them,
delicate, pretty, bullying flowers of gloom.
I can't look at them.

The bluebells will come
every year
and I despise them.

I wish you lived next door

I wish you lived next door
and every day we saw
each other more and more....
but only in short bursts
and not in any routine or pattern
because although, at times, reassuring,
routine quickly becomes mundane,
thoughtlessly and inevitably sliding into
convenience,
ending acrimoniously with a clumsy crash
landing and exorbitant fees.
If you lived next door
we would pop into each other and ask nicely to
borrow cups of sugar or a slice of bread.
We could meet for breakfast before work,
and return to our own homes at the end of a busy
day
not begrudgingly, to wash up or pick up lazily
abandoned socks,
nor to be in exhausted competition about who
has had the busiest day,
but to knock politely on next doors door and
to tenderly and genuinely enjoy an independent
kiss, a sincere touch, a not taken for granted
cuddle.

We could order a takeaway and casually stick a
head into the adjourning porch
to invite the other for supper, conversation, and
an after-dinner foot rub.
We could go home quickly to our own cosy bed
and sleep soundly
comfortable with the knowledge that a simple
wall separates us and not a stretch of the A394
and B3280
8.1 miles of missing you...
and in our own contentment we would be the
correct temperature
with the whole duvet or none of it,
spread out or curled up
2 pillows or 1 or none.
If you lived next door
you would ask me out on dates, drives,
picnics, trips to the cinema, walks…
and I would dress up.
We would make the effort to see each other
and we would... we could... every day.
But you don't live next door and neither do I
and living apart is beautiful
geographic distance traversed by honest
affection
bridged by love
and fresh desire delivered each day
to our doorsteps, like milk.

Resolve

She couldn't do it anymore
her arms ached, her legs were sore
she pressed her head against the door
and pushed her feet into the floor
she knew she had to win the war
tiredness spreading from her core
resolve, she said, you've got til four
when he'll be back, demanding more
pack your bags, you can't ignore
your self, your being, self abhor
you fucking whore
take it no more
get out right now, but not before
you hurl the glass onto the floor
that bruise is bigger, getting sore
it's time to leave, forget the score
your lip is swelling, the neighbour saw
he didn't like the dress you wore
so leave the house
and leave the noise
go now, you know you have the choice
you're strong
you're fierce
you're full of fire
go now
before you get too tired.

Make sure nothing is wasted

we don't have a time machine
so hold them close and keep them precious
say the words and
see the signs
the exquisite signs of those we miss;
the picture drawn when they were four
the dusty award from ballet school
the crumpled certificates, the brownie badges,
the provisional driving licence
the smell of their suitcase
the hair in their brush
the favourite book, corners turned at the best bits
the mother's day card saying I love you…
hold them close and keep them precious
and make sure nothing is wasted.

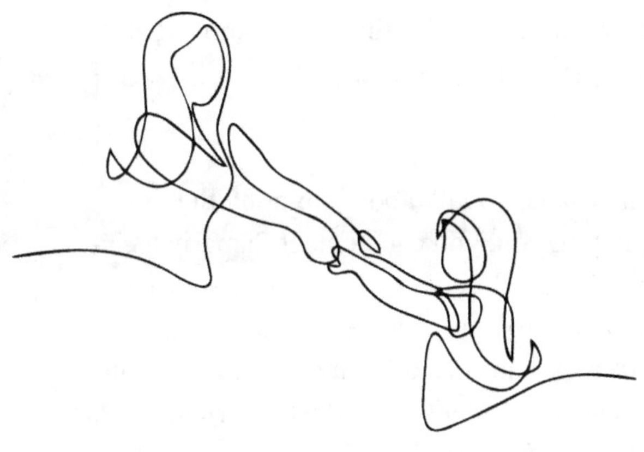

Pick up the phone

One or more of these themes might have
triggered something in you...
Use the people and organisations in this list;
they're all great, and you might feel better
getting the shitty stuff out of your brain and off
your chest. Or write it all down. Either way,
acknowledge the shit things and know that it's
OK to shout about them.
With love x

Samaritans. To talk about anything that is
upsetting you, you can contact Samaritans 24
hours a day, 365 days a year. You can call 116
123 (free from any phone), email
jo@samaritans.org or visit some branches in
person. You can also call the Samaritans Welsh
Language Line on 0808 164 0123 (7pm–11pm
every day).
SANEline. If you're experiencing a mental
health problem or supporting someone else, you
can call SANEline on 0300 304 7000
(4.30pm–10.30pm every day).
National Suicide Prevention Helpline UK.
Offers a supportive listening service to anyone
with thoughts of suicide. You can call the

National Suicide Prevention Helpline UK on
0800 689 5652 (open 24/7).
Campaign Against Living Miserably (CALM).
You can call the CALM on 0800 58 58 58
(5pm–midnight every day) if you are struggling
and need to talk. Or if you prefer not to speak on
the phone, you could try the CALM webchat
service.
Shout. If you would prefer not to talk but want
some mental health support, you could text
SHOUT to 85258. Shout offers a confidential
24/7 text service providing support if you are in
crisis and need immediate help.
The Mix. If you're under 25, you can call The
Mix on 0808 808 4994 (3pm–midnight every
day), request support by email using this form
on The Mix website or use their crisis text
messenger service.
Papyrus HOPELINEUK. If you're under 35 and
struggling with suicidal feelings, or concerned
about a young person who might be struggling,
you can call Papyrus HOPELINEUK on 0800
068 4141 (weekdays 10am-10pm, weekends
2pm-10pm and bank holidays 2pm–10pm),
email pat@papyrus-uk.org or text 07786 209
697.
Nightline. If you're a student, you can look on
the Nightline website to see if your university or

college offers a night-time listening service. Nightline phone operators are all students too. Switchboard. If you identify as gay, lesbian, bisexual or transgender, you can call Switchboard on 0300 330 0630 (10am–10pm every day), email chris@switchboard.lgbt or use their webchat service. Phone operators all identify as LGBT+.

C.A.L.L. If you live in Wales, you can call the Community Advice and Listening Line (C.A.L.L.) on 0800 132 737 (open 24/7) or you can text 'help' followed by a question to 81066.

Helplines Partnership. For more options, visit the Helplines Partnership website for a directory of UK helplines. Mind's Infoline can also help you find services that can support you. If you're outside the UK, the Befrienders Worldwide website has a tool to search by country for emotional support helplines around the world.

Cruse Bereavement Care; www.cruse.org.uk; helpline@cruse.org.uk; 0808 808 1677
Helpline opening hours: Monday - Friday 9.30am - 5pm (excluding bank holidays) with extended hours on Tuesdays, Wednesdays and Thursdays to 8pm
Young People's website: hopeagain.org.uk
Miscarriage Association; 01924 200799; www.miscarriageassociation.org.uk

Stillbirth and Neonatal Death Society (SANDS);
0808 164 3332; helpline@sands.org.uk;
www.sands.org.uk
Child Bereavement UK; 0800 028 8840 for the
Information & Support Team;
www.childbereavementuk.org
TCF (formerly The Compassionate Friends);
0845 123 2304 (Every day of the year 10am to
4pm and 6.30pm to 10.30pm); www.tcf.org.uk
Support by telephone, befriending and local
groups for anyone affected by the death of a
child. Please note that this charity supports
people irrespective of the age of the child at the
time of death i.e. the child may have reached
adulthood.
Carers Trust; The new organisation for carers
formed by the merging of Crossroad Care and
the Princess Royal Trust for Carers. (The
Princess Royal Trust for Carers is still the title in
Scotland). Find support in your area; if you
cannot find what you want on the website call
this number: 0800 800 4361